MICKEY'S PRACTICE WORKBOOKS

ADDITION AND SUBTRACTION

By Margery Altman
Illustrated by Walt Disney Productions

ISBN: 0-448-16124-9

Published by WONDER BOOKS

A Division of Grosset & Dunlap
A Filmways Company
Publishers · New York

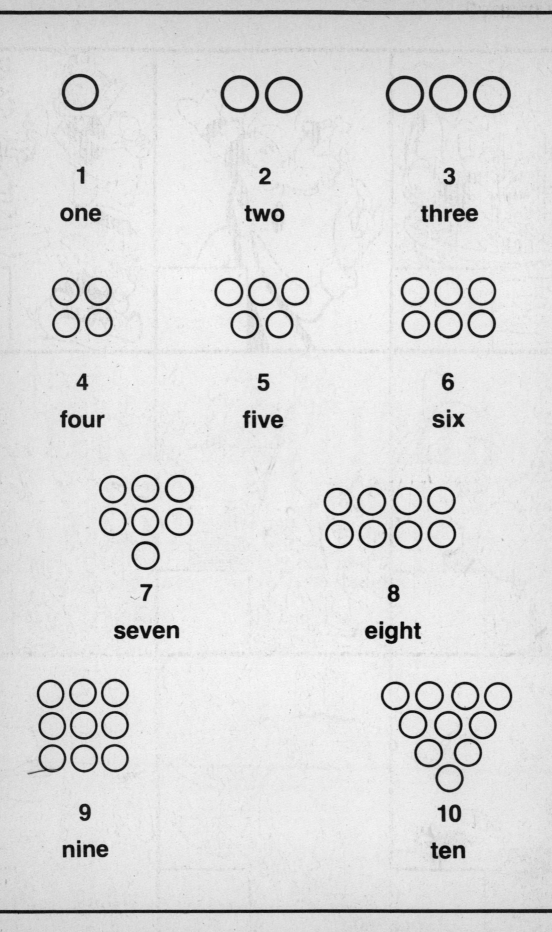

How many?

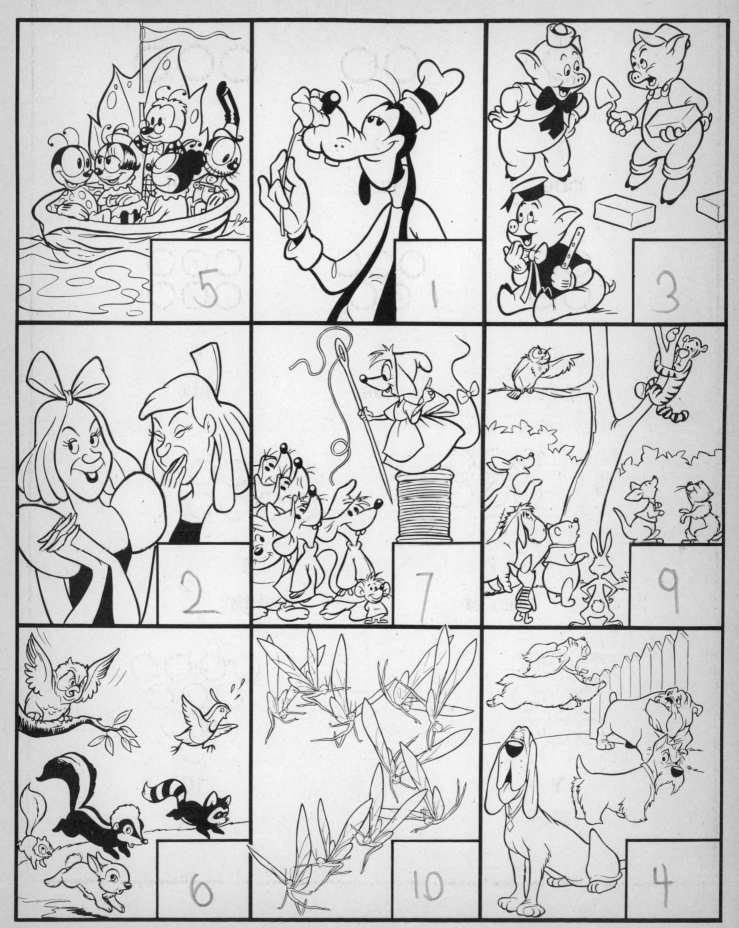

one
one

1

Here is one duck.　1

Circle the ones.

two
two

2

Here are two dogs. 2

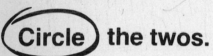 the twos.

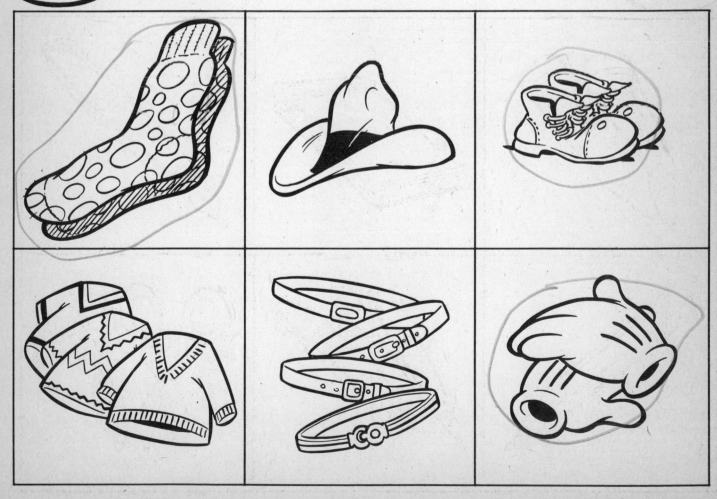

three
three

3

Here are three mice.   3

(Circle) the threes.

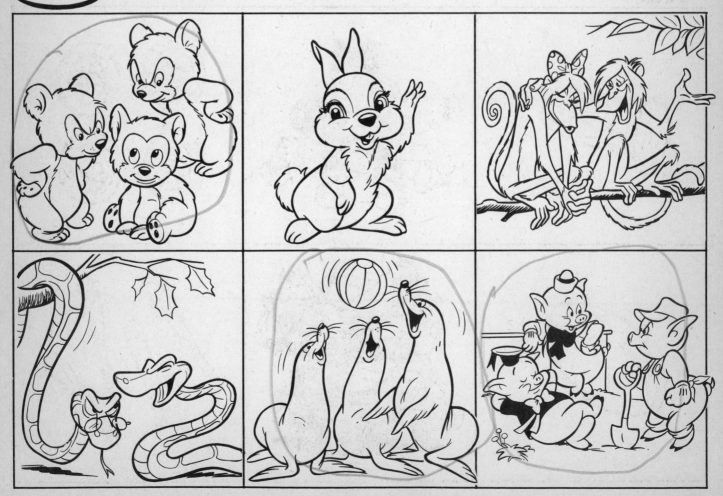

four
four

4

Here are four fairies. 4

Circle the fours.

five
five

5

Here are five dinosaurs.   5

(Circle) the fives.

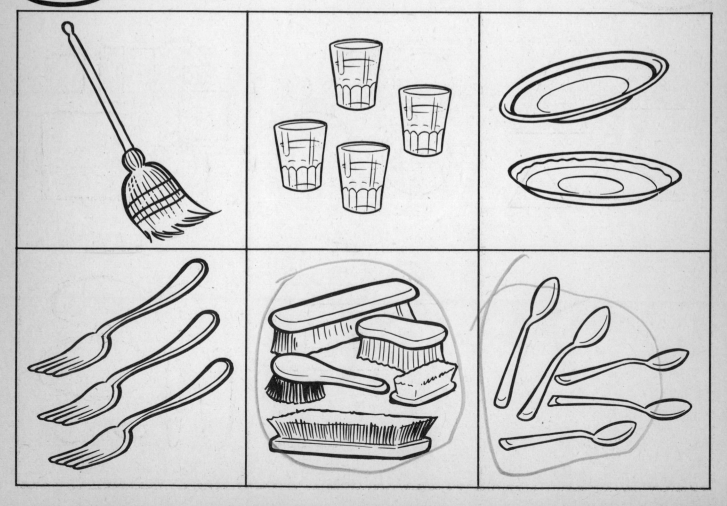

six
six

6

Here are six elephants.   6

⬭ Circle ⬭ the sixes.

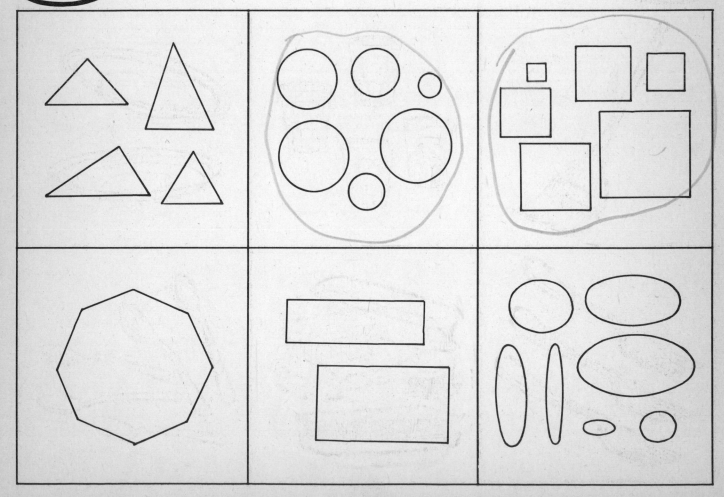

seven
seven
7

Here are seven dwarfs.   7

Circle the sevens.

eight
eight

8

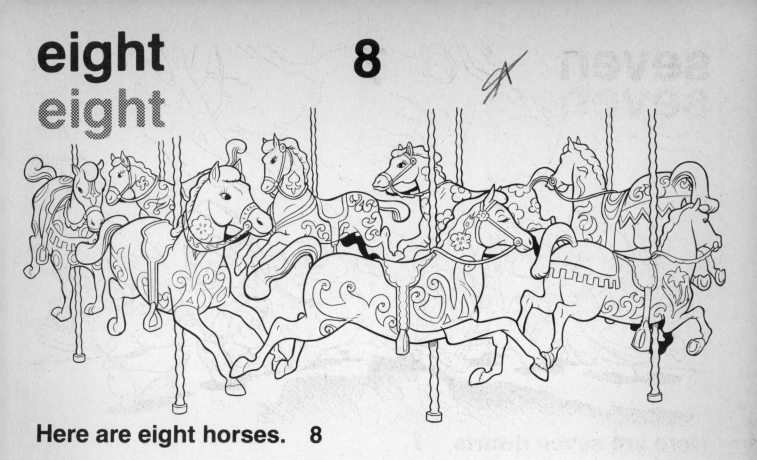

Here are eight horses.   8

Circle the eights.

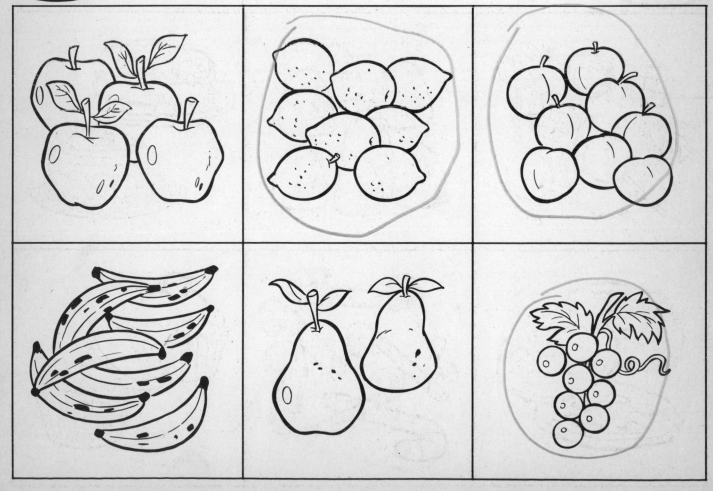

nine
nine

9

Here are nine puppies.   9

Circle the nines.

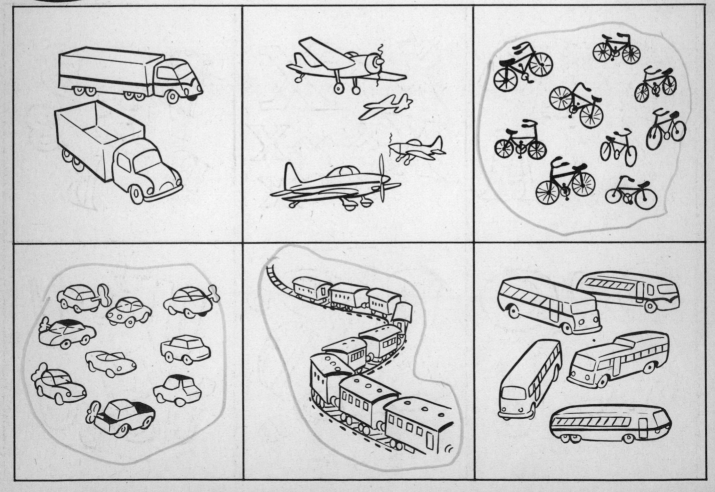

ten
ten

Here are ten animals.   10

(Circle) **the tens.**

Write the number words.

Match the words.

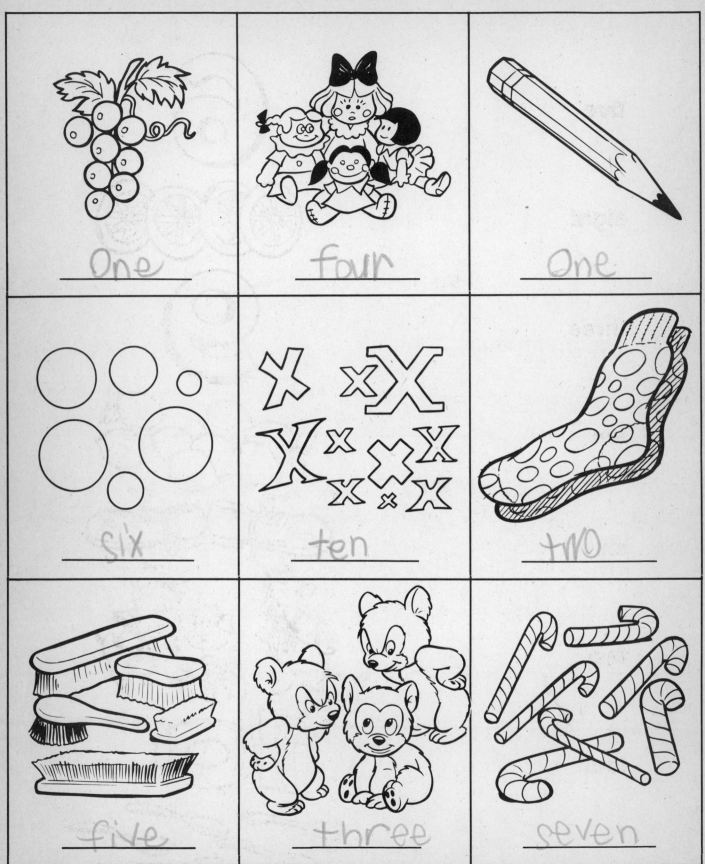

one ___
four ___
one ___
six ___
ten ___
two ___
five ___
three ___
seven ___

one two three four five six seven eight nine ten

Match the words.

five

eight

three

ten

six

two

four

nine

Here is one fairy.

$1 + 0 = \underline{1}$

$\underline{1} + 0 = 1$

Here are two fairies. 2

$1 + 1 = \underline{2}$

$\underline{3} + 1 = 2$

Draw one more fairy.

$2 + 1 = \underline{3}$

$\underline{4} + 1 = 3$

Write the numbers.

✿ + ✿ = ✿✿

$\underline{One} + \underline{one} = \underline{two}$

✿✿✿ + ✿ = ✿✿✿✿

$\underline{three} + \underline{One} = \underline{four}$

Here are two thistle boys. $\boxed{2}$

$2 + 0 = 2$

$\underline{1} + \underline{1} = 2$

Write the numbers.

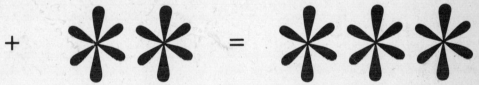

$\underline{\text{One}} + \underline{\text{two}} = \underline{\text{three}}$

$\underline{\text{two}} + \underline{\text{two}} = \underline{\text{four}}$

$\underline{\text{four}} + \underline{\text{two}} = \underline{\text{six}}$

Here are three puppets. 3

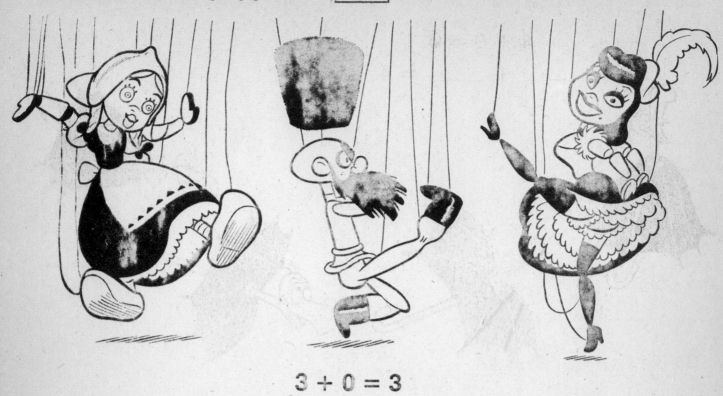

$$3 + 0 = 3$$
$$\underline{} + \underline{} = 3$$

Write the numbers.

one + three = four

three + three = six

Here are four birds.

$$4 + 0 = 4$$
$$\underline{\hspace} + \underline{\hspace} = 4$$

Write the numbers.

One + four = five

three + four = seven

Here are five chickens. $\boxed{5}$

Write the number.

$$5 + 0 = 5$$
$$\underline{0} + \underline{5} = 5$$

Write the numbers.

$\triangledown$ + $\triangle\triangledown\triangle\triangle\triangleright$ = $\triangle\triangledown\triangle\triangledown\triangle\triangledown\triangleright$

$\underline{\text{one}}$ + $\underline{\text{five}}$ = $\underline{\text{six}}$

$\triangle\triangledown\triangleright$ + $\triangle\triangledown\triangledown\triangle\triangledown$ = $\triangle\triangle\triangle\triangledown\triangle\triangledown\triangle\triangledown$

$\underline{\text{three}}$ + $\underline{\text{five}}$ = $\underline{\text{eight}}$

Write the numbers.

◖◗ ◖ + ◗ __five__	✱✱✱ + ✱ __four__	✱ ✱ + ✱ __three__
✱ ✱ + ✱ ✱ __four__	◗ + ◖◗ __five__	✱ + ✱ __two__
◗◗ ◗ + ◗ __five__	✱ ✱ ✱ ✱ + ✱ ✱ __six__	✱✱✱ + ✱✱✱ ✱✱ __eight__

Here are six geese. $\boxed{6}$

$$6 + 0 = 6$$
$$\underline{0} + \underline{6} = 6$$

Write the numbers.

✗ + ✗✗✗ / ✗✗✗ = ✗✗✗✗ / ✗✗✗

<u>one</u> + <u>six</u> = <u>seven</u>

✗✗ / ✗✗ + ✗✗✗ / ✗✗✗ = ✗✗✗✗✗ / ✗✗✗✗✗

<u>four</u> + <u>six</u> = <u>ten</u>

Here are seven mice.

$$7 + 0 = 7$$
$$0 + 7 = 7$$

Write the numbers.

● + ●●●● ●●● = ●●●● ●●●

one + seven = eight

●●● + ●●●● ●●● = ●●●●● ●●●●●

three + seven = ten

Here are eight bats.

$$8 + 0 = 8$$
$$\underline{0} + \underline{8} = 8$$

Write the numbers.

▼ + ▼▼▼▼▼▼▼ = ▼▼▼▼▼▼▼▼

one + eight = nine

▼▼ + ▼▼▼▼▼▼ = ▼▼▼▼▼▼▼▼

two + eight = ten

Here are nine sailors.
9

$$9 + 0 = 9$$
$$\underline{0} + \underline{9} = 9$$

Write the numbers.

◇ + ◇◇◇◇◇ ◇◇◇◇ = ◇◇◇◇◇ ◇◇◇◇

__one__ + __nine__ = __ten__

◇◇◇ + ◇◇◇◇◇ ◇◇◇◇ = ◇◇◇◇◇◇ ◇◇◇◇◇◇

__three__ + __nine__ = __twelv__

Here are ten Indians. 10

$$0 + 10 = 10$$
$$\underline{10} + \underline{0} = 10$$

Write the numbers.

●●●   +   ●●●●●   =   ●●●●●
●●   ●●●●●   ●●●●●

five + _ten_ = _fiften_

●●   +   ●●●●●   =   ●●●●●
         ●●●●●   ●●●●
●●●

two + _ten_ = _twelv_

Write the numbers.

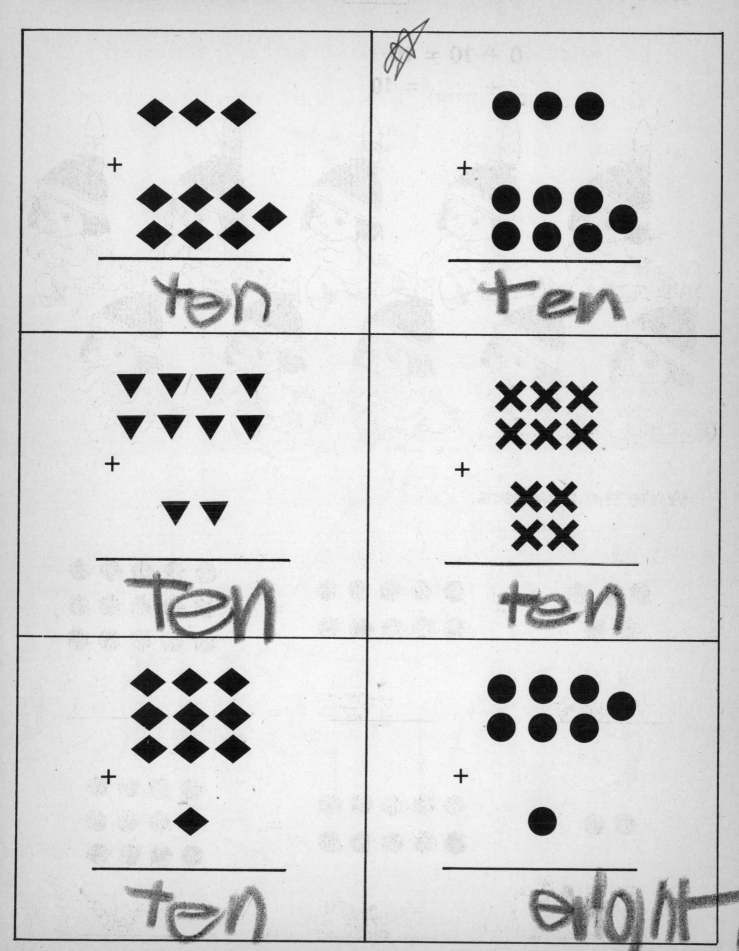

ten

ten

ten

ten

ten

eight

Alice found something. She doesn't know what it is. Help her. First, find the sums. Then start with 1. Go in number order. Draw a line to the circles. What does Alice have? 1234567896

0 + 1 = __1__

__10__ = 6 + 4

1 + 1 = __2__ ◯

2 + 1 = __3__ ◯   ◯ __9__ = 4 + 5

2 + 2 = __4__ ◯

2 + 3 = __5__ ◯

4 + 2 = __6__ ◯   ◯ __8__ = 5 + 3

3 + 4 = __7__ ◯

Each batter scored some runs.
Write the sum on each bat.

Build Humpty Dumpty's wall.
Write the missing numbers in each block.

$1 + 1 = 1$

$1 + 1 = 2$ | $0 + 2 = 2$

$0 + 3 = 3$ | $2 + 1 = 3$ | $1 + 2 =$

$0 + 4 = 4$ | $2 + 2 = 4$ | $3 + 1 = 4$

$1 + 4 = 5$ | $2 + 3 = 5$ | $0 + 5 = 5$

$3 + 3 = 6$ | $2 + 4 = 6$ | $1 + 5 = 6$

$4 + 3 = 7$ | $1 + 6 = 7$ | $2 + 5 = 7$ | $7 + 0 =$

$2 + 6 = 8$ | $4 + 4 = 8$ | $5 + 3 = 8$ | $0 + 8 = 8$

$6 + 3 = 9$ | $4 + 5 = 9$ | $2 + 8 = 9$

$1 + 8 = 9$ | $0 + 9 = 9$

$5 + 5 = 10$ | $1 + 9 = 10$ | $2 + 8 = 10$ | $3 + 7 = 10$

$4 + 6 = 10$

1 + **3** = 4

4 + **1** = 5   3 + **2** = 5

6 + **0** = 6   4 + **2** = 6   **1** + 5 = 6

1 + **6** = 7   3 + **4** = 7   5 + **2** = 7

1 + **7** = 8   **6** + 2 = 8   3 + **5** = 8   **4** + 4 = 8

6 + **3** = 9   5 + **4** = 9   **2** + 7 = 9   1 + **8** = 9

0 + **10** = 10   **5** + 5 = 10

7 + **3** = 10   4 + **6** = 10

**Find the sum on each sheep.
Draw a line from each sheep to
the correct number pen.**

4

0 + 4 = 4

3 + 2 = 5

1 + 2 = 3

1 + 4 = 5

3 + 0 = 3

$3 + 1 = 4$

$2 + 2 = 4$

$5 + 0 = 5$

5

$1 + 3 = 4$

3

$0 + 3 = 3$

Find the sum in each egg.
Draw a line from each egg to the correct number nest.

8

3 + 5 = 8

4 + 2 = 6

3 + 3 = 6

1 + 6 = 7

5 + 1 = 6

4 + 3 = 7

6

4 + 4 = 8

0 + 6 = 6

5 + 2 = 7

7

8 + 0 = 8

2 + 6 = 8

0 + 7 = 7

Find the sum on each pumpkin.

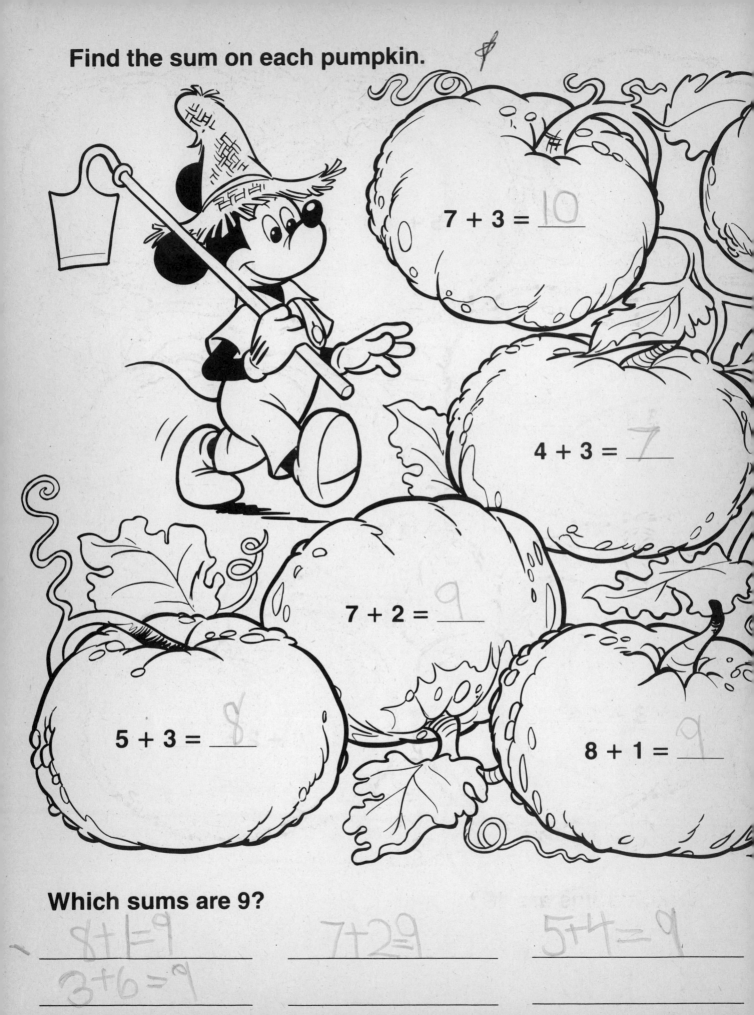

$7 + 3 = \underline{10}$

$4 + 3 = \underline{7}$

$7 + 2 = \underline{9}$

$5 + 3 = \underline{8}$

$8 + 1 = \underline{9}$

Which sums are 9?

$8+1=9$

$7+2=9$

$5+4=9$

$3+6=9$

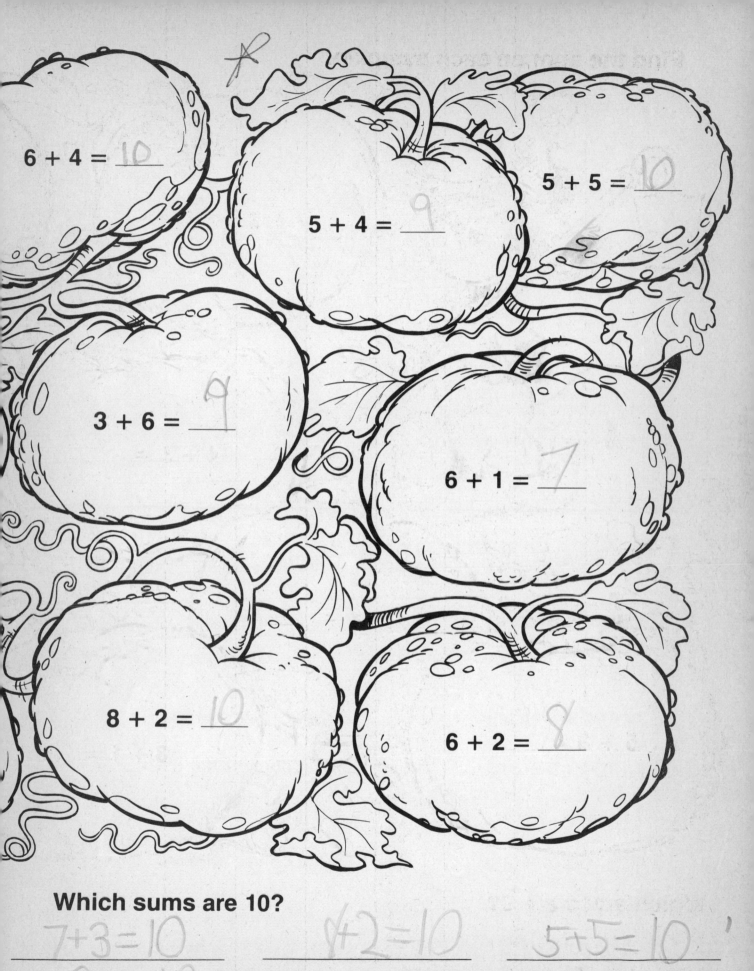

$6 + 4 = \underline{10}$

$5 + 4 = \underline{9}$

$5 + 5 = \underline{10}$

$3 + 6 = \underline{9}$

$6 + 1 = \underline{7}$

$8 + 2 = \underline{10}$

$6 + 2 = \underline{8}$

Which sums are 10?

$7 + 3 = 10$ $8 + 2 = 10$ $5 + 5 = 10$

$6 + 4 = 10$

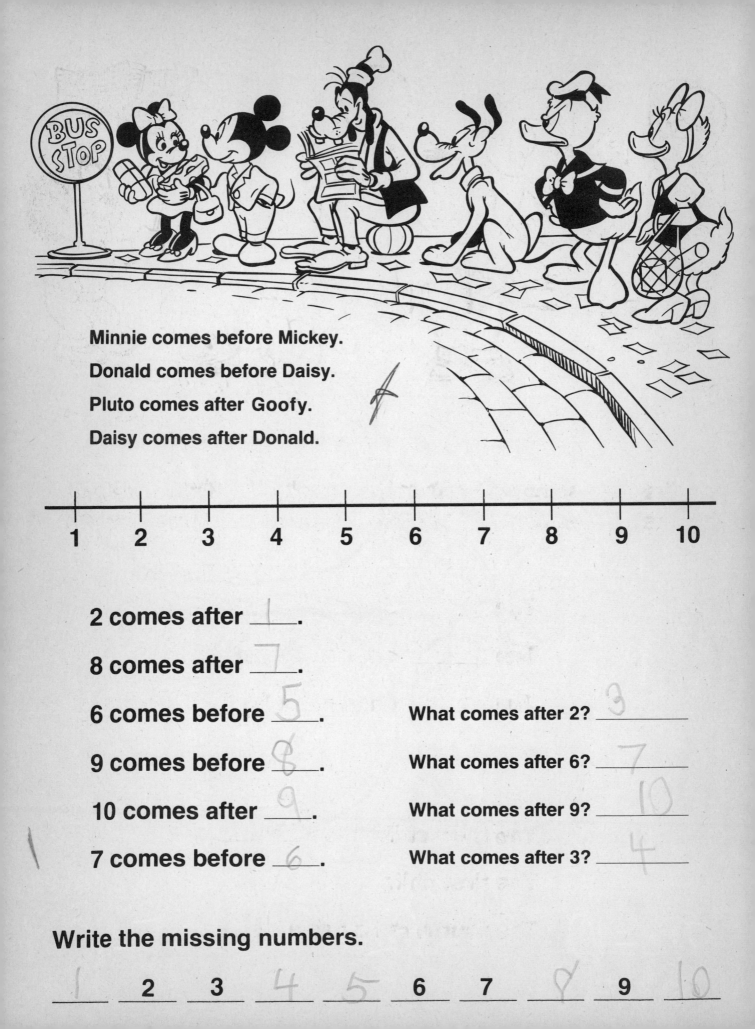

Minnie comes before Mickey.

Donald comes before Daisy.

Pluto comes after Goofy.

Daisy comes after Donald.

1 2 3 4 5 6 7 8 9 10

2 comes after __1__.

8 comes after __7__.

6 comes before __5__.   What comes after 2? __3__

9 comes before __8__.   What comes after 6? __7__

10 comes after __9__.   What comes after 9? __10__

7 comes before __6__.   What comes after 3? __4__

Write the missing numbers.

__1__ 2 3 __4__ __5__ 6 7 __8__ 9 __10__

first	second	third	fourth	fifth	sixth
first	second	third	fourth	fifth	sixth

The _second_ child has a kite.

The _fifth_ child has a cat.

The _sixth_ child has a flag.

The third child has a _hat_.

The first child has a _book_.

The fourth child has a _ball_.

Write the missing numbers.

1	2	3	4	5	6	7	8	9	10
11	12	13	14	15	16	17	18	19	20
21	22	23	24	25	26	27	28	29	30
31	32	33	34	35	36	37	38	39	40
41	42	43	44	45	46	47	48	49	50
51	52	53	54	55	56	57	58	59	60
61	62	63	64	65	66	67	68	69	70
71	72	73	74	75	76	77	78	79	80
81	82	83	84	85	86	87	88	89	90
91	92	93	94	95	96	97	98	99	100

Write the numbers.

20 __21__ __22__ __23__
__24__ __25__ __26__ __27__
__28__ **29**

__50__ __51__ __52__ __53__
__54__ __55__ **56** __57__
__58__ __59__

__30__ __31__ **32** __33__
34 __35__ __36__ __37__
__38__ __39__

90 __91__ __92__ __93__
__94__ **95** __96__ __97__
__98__ __99__

Here are two turtles. ⬚2

   One walks away. ⬚1

   One is left. ⬚1

     $2 - 1 = \underline{1}$

Write the numbers.

■ ■ ■   –   ■   =   ■ ■

three – _one_ = _two_

■ ■ ■
■ ■   –   ■   =   ■ ■ ■ ■

five – _one_ = _four_

Here are three hippos. ☐3

Two walk away. ☐2

One is left. ☐1

$3 - 2 = 1$

Write the numbers.

● ● ● ● − ● ● = ● ●

four − two = two

● ● ●
● ● ● − ● ● ● = ● ● ● ●

six − two = four

Write the numbers.

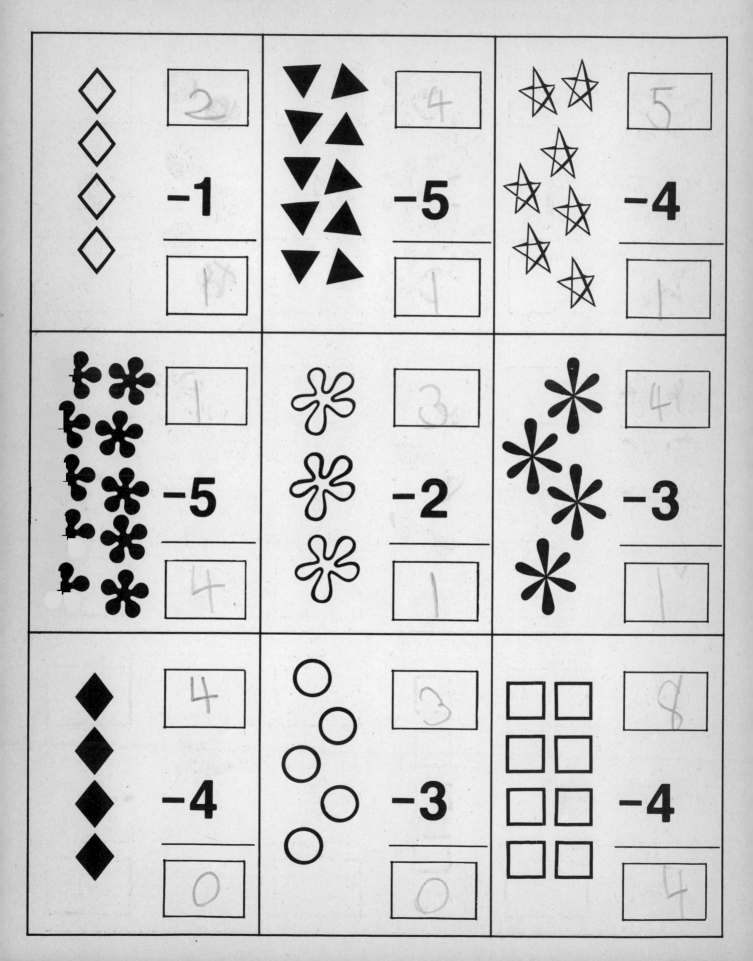

-1   2 / 4

-5   4 / 1

-4   5 / 1

-5   1 / 4

-2   3 / 1

-3   4 / 1

-4   4 / 0

-3   3 / 0

-4   8 / 4

Write the numbers.

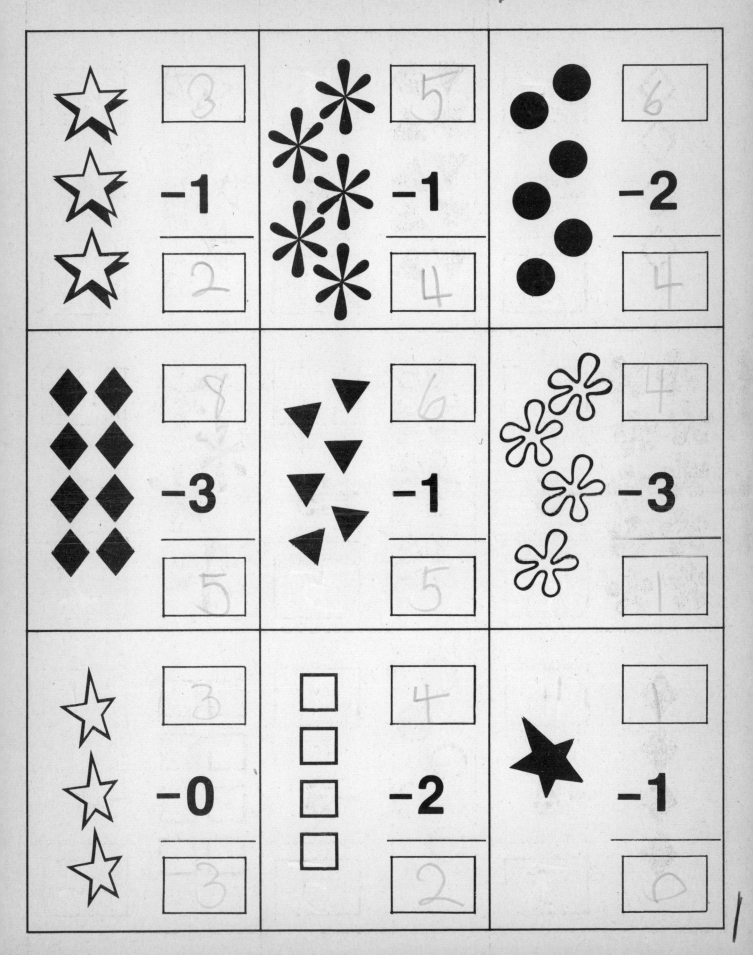

Write the numbers.

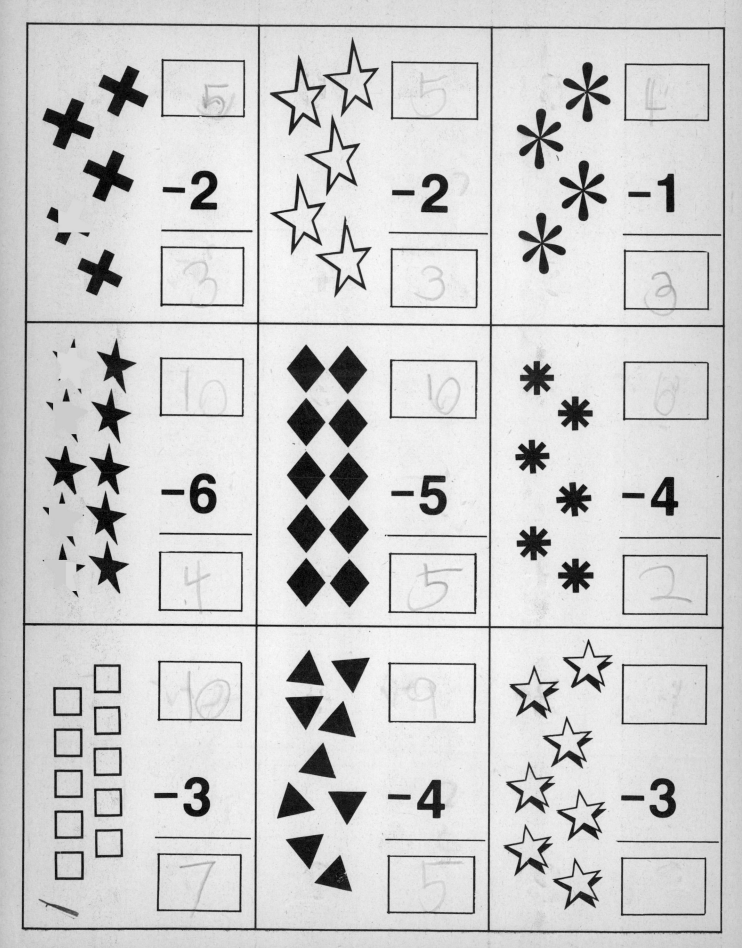

5	−2	3	5	−2	3
10	−6	4	10	−5	5
10	−3	7	9	−4	5

4	−1	3
6	−4	2
7	−3	

Write the numbers.

○○ ○○ ○○ ○○ **8** — 3 5	▲▲ ▲▲ ▲▲ ▲▲ ▲▲ **10** — 6 4	✖✖ ✖ ✖ ✖ **5** — 4 1
✱✱ ✱✱ ✱✱ ✱ **7** — 2 5	▽▽ ▽▽ ▽▽ ▽ **9** — 3 6	☆☆ ☆☆ ☆☆ ☆☆ ☆ **9** — 0 9
❂❂ ❂❂ ❂❂ ❂❂ ❂ **9** — 7 2	◆◆ ◆◆ ◆◆ **8** — 1 7	★★ ★★ ★★ ★ **5** — 4 1

Write the numbers.

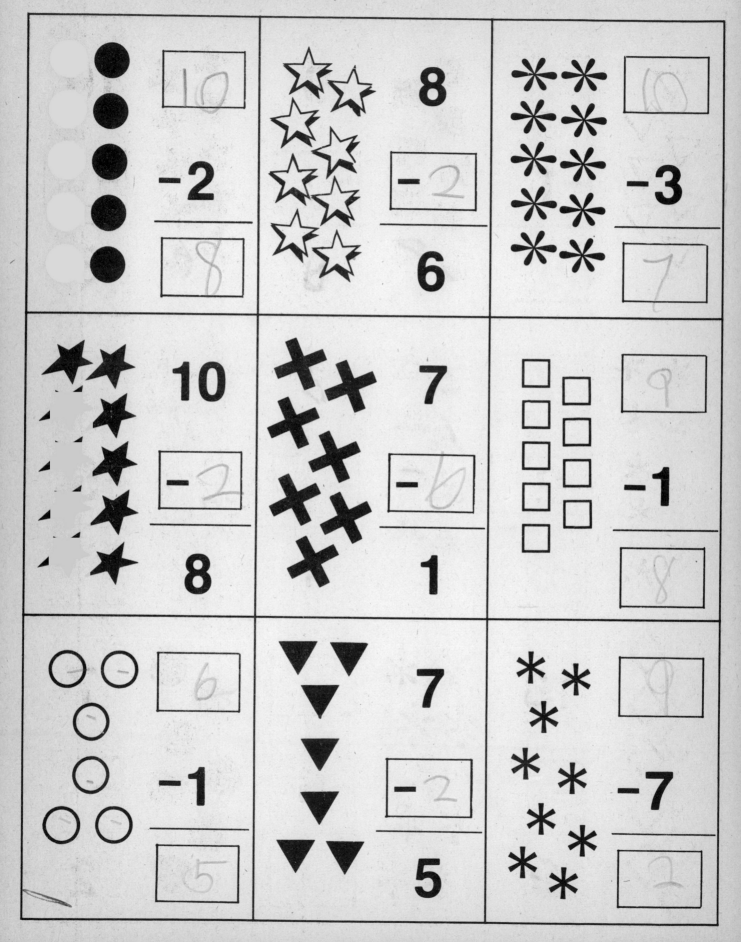

10 −2 8	8 −2 6	10 −3 7
10 −2 8	7 −6 1	9 −1 8
6 −1 5	7 −2 5	9 −7 2

Write the numbers.

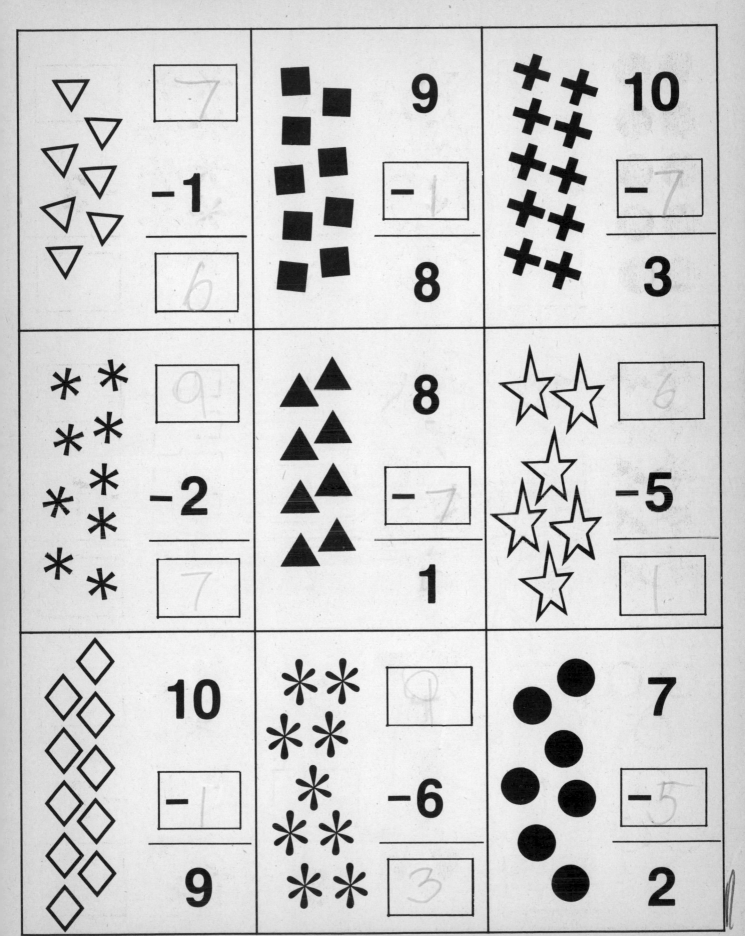

Help the Ringmaster start the show. Find the sum on each elephant. Draw a line from each elephant to the correct number ring.

7 – 6 =

1

10 – 9 = 1

8 – 6 =

Help the Prince make his way through the forest. He must find Snow White. Cut down any tree with a wrong number. Show the Prince's path through the forest.

The dog catcher will catch all the dogs with correct answers. (Circle) **the dogs he will not catch.**

$8-6=2$

$9-6=4$

$10-5=4$

$10-7=2$

$4-1=2$

$3-2=1$

$5-2=2$

$7-4=3$

$8-3=5$

$7-2=5$

Captain Hook must walk the plank. Help him cross the crocodiles' lake. Write the number in the spaces.

1 − 0 = 1

1 − 1 = 0

2 − 2 = 0

2 − 1 = 1

2 − 0 = 2

3 − 0 = 3

3 − 1 = 2

3 − 2 = 1

3 − 3 = 0

4 − 0 =

4 − 1 =

4 − 2 =

4 − 3 =

4 − 4 =

$10 - 0 = 10$

$9 - 0 = 9$

$8 - 0 = 8$

$10 - 1 = 9$

$7 - 0 = 7$

$9 - 1 = 8$

$8 - 1 = 7$

$10 - 2 = 8$

$6 - 0 = 6$

$9 - 2 = 7$

$7 - 1 = 6$

$8 - 2 = 6$

$10 - 3 = 7$

$- 0 = 5$

$6 - 1 = 5$

$9 - 3 = 6$

$7 - 2 = 5$

$8 - 3 = 5$

$10 - 4 = 6$

$- 1 = 4$

$6 - 2 = 4$

$8 - 4 = 4$

$7 - 3 = 4$

$9 - 4 = 5$

$10 - 5 = 5$

$- 2 = 3$

$6 - 3 = 3$

$7 - 4 = 3$

$8 - 5 = 3$

$9 - 5 = 4$

$10 - 6 = 4$

$- 3 = 2$

$6 - 4 = 2$

$7 - 5 = 2$

$9 - 6 = 3$

$8 - 6 = 3$

$- 4 = 1$

$6 - 5 = 1$

$10 - 7 = 3$

$7 - 6 = 1$

$8 - 7 = 1$

$9 - 7 = 2$

$- 5 = 0$

$10 - 8 = 2$

$6 - 6 = 0$

$9 - 8 = 1$

$7 - 7 = 0$

$8 - 8 = 0$

$10 - 9 = 1$

$9 - 9 = 0$

$10 - 10 = 0$

Some shoes will fit each girl.
You can find out which ones they are.
Each answer will be a shoe size.
Color Cinderella's shoes red.
Color Anastasia's shoes green.
Color Drizella's shoes yellow.
Color Stepmother's shoes blue.

size 6

size 7

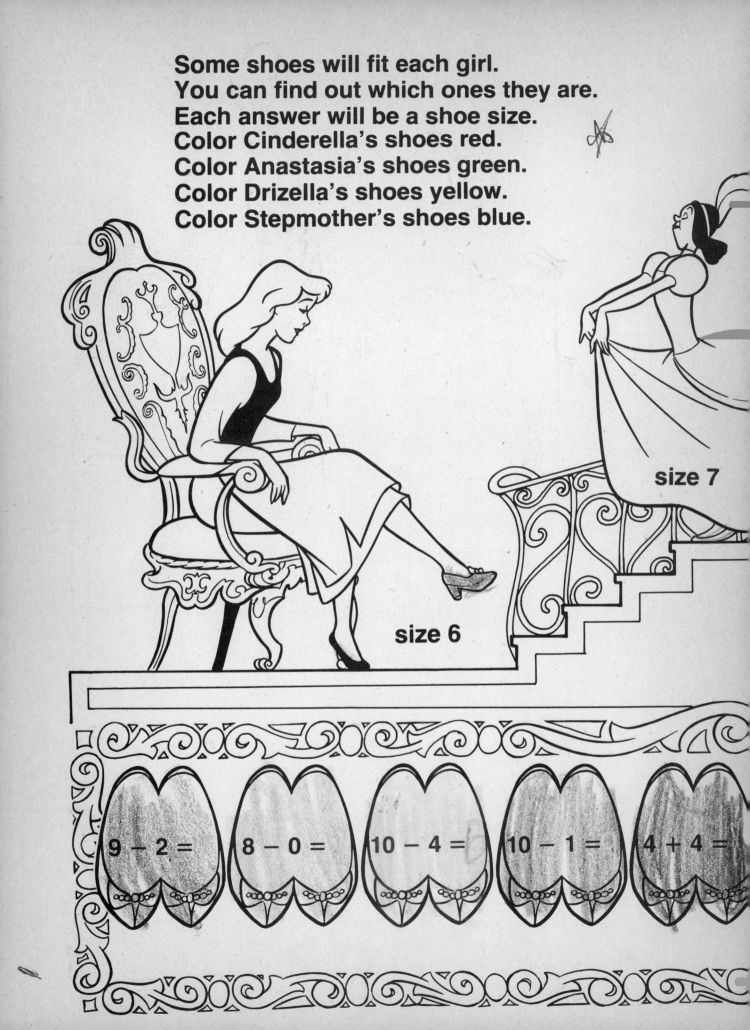

$9 - 2 =$ $8 - 0 =$ $10 - 4 =$ $10 - 1 =$ $4 + 4 =$

size 8

size 9

8 + 1 =   6 + 2 =   5 + 2 =   5 + 1 =   3 + 3 =

Go with Mickey Mouse to the head of the class.
Write the numbers on each book.

2 + 2 = 4

5 − 4 = 1

10 − 2 = 3

3 + 1 = 4

6 − 3 = 3

2 + 6 = 8

4 − 2 = 2

6 − 2 = 4

1 + 9 = 10

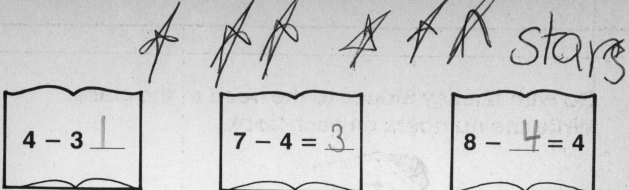

stars

4 − 3 <u>1</u>

7 − 4 = 3

8 − <u>4</u> = 4

3 + 2 = <u>5</u>

5 + 2 = <u>7</u>

5 + <u>3</u> = 8

4 + <u>5</u> = 9

<u>5</u> + 5 = 10

<u>2</u> − 4 = 2

9 − <u>3</u> = 6

<u>7</u> − 1 = 6

<u>2</u> − 5 = 3

6 + <u>2</u> = 8

<u>4</u> + 5 = 9

<u>0</u> + 4 = 4

7 − <u>4</u> = 3

<u>6</u> + 4 = 10

<u>8</u> + 1 = 9

The Mad Hatter must buy things for his party. Help him in the store. He paid for each thing with a dime (10¢). How much change will he get back for each thing?

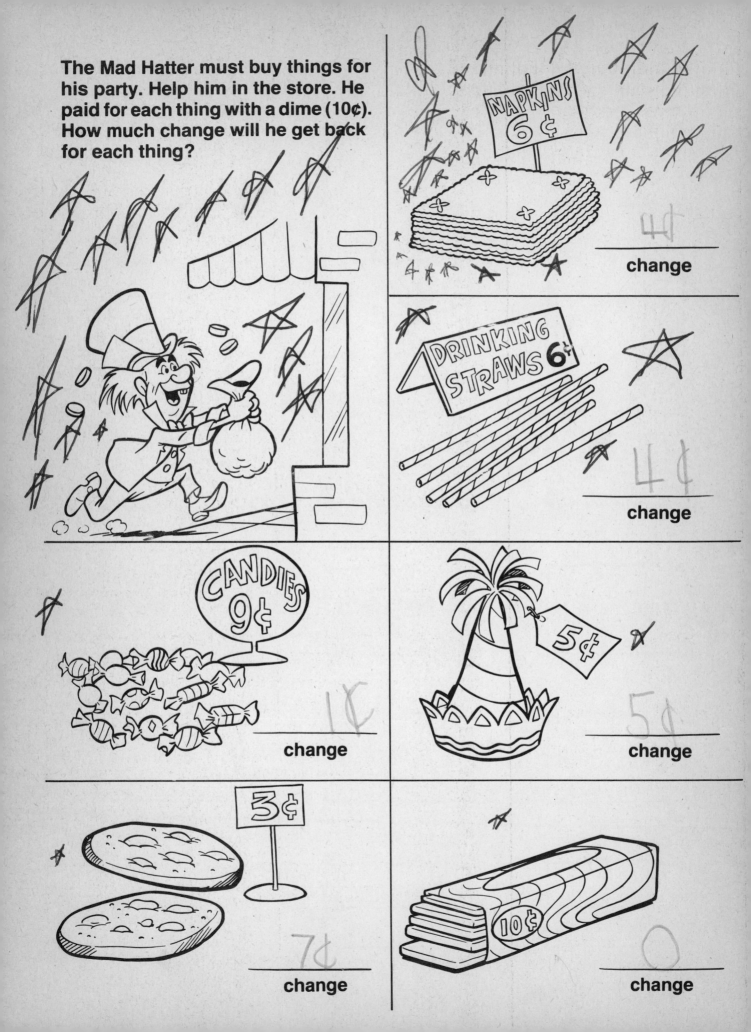

NAPKINS 6¢

4¢

change

DRINKING STRAWS 6¢

4¢

change

CANDIES 9¢

1¢

change

5¢

5¢

change

3¢

7¢

change

10¢

0

change